Evan Hause

Fields

for 5-octave Marimba

Fields explores and celebrates the wide-openness and free-spiritedness
on the inside and outside of us. It was performed on November 2, 1991
in Warner Concert Hall at the Oberlin Conservatory by Loren Mach.

ISBN 978-1-4950-0963-1

EDWARD B. MARKS MUSIC COMPANY

EXCLUSIVELY DISTRIBUTED BY

HAL•LEONARD® CORPORATION
7777 W. BLUEMOUND RD. P.O. BOX 13819 MILWAUKEE, WI 53213

www.ebmarks.com
www.halleonard.com

Dedicated to Michael Rosen

FIELDS

I

Evan Hause

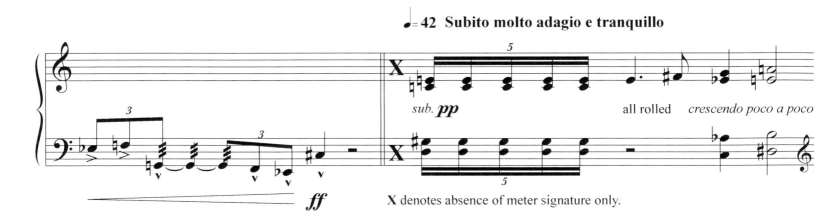

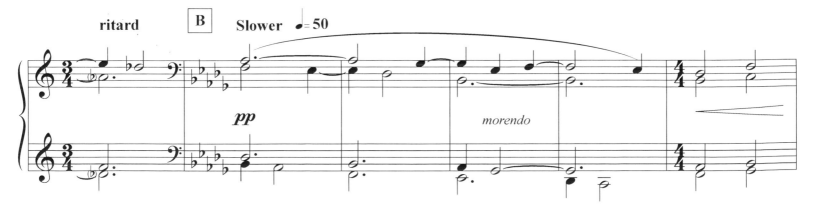

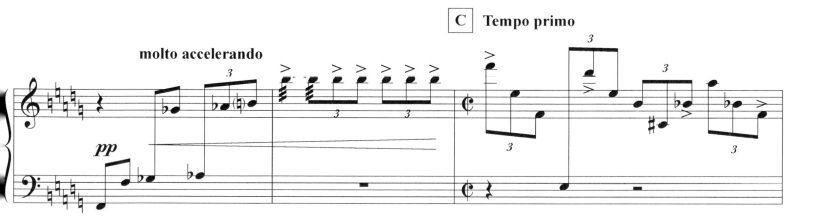

C Tempo primo

molto accelerando

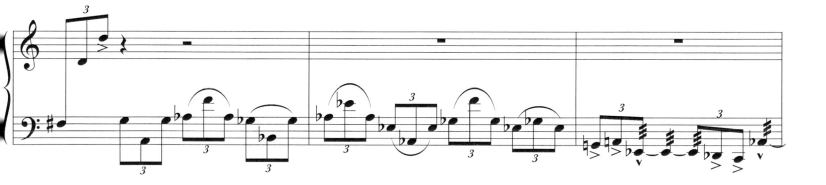

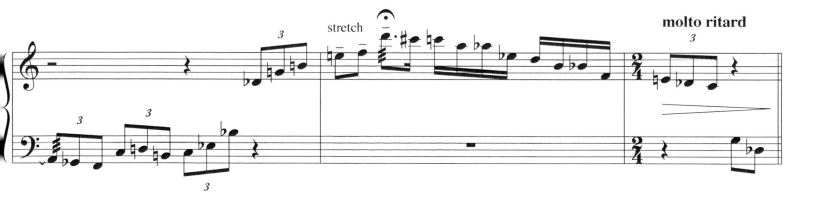

stretch

molto ritard

4

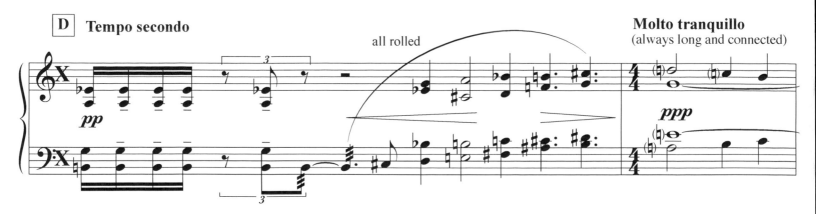

D **Tempo secondo**

all rolled

Molto tranquillo
(always long and connected)

pp

ppp

E

begin slowly and accelerate steadily

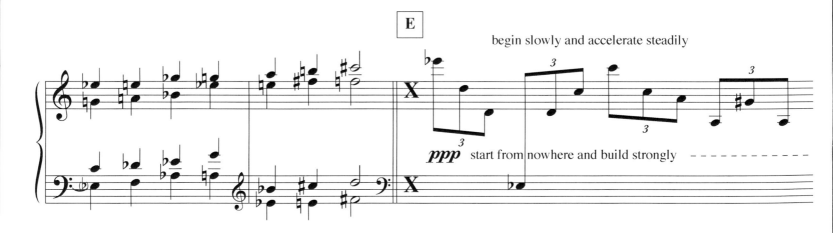

ppp start from nowhere and build strongly - - - - - - - - - - - - -

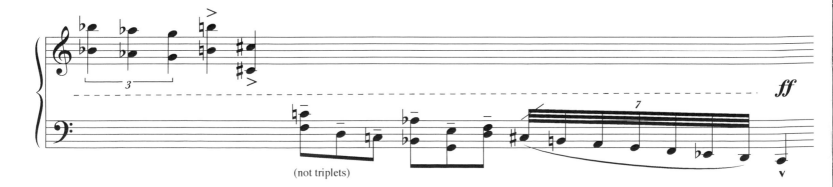

(not triplets)

ff

very fast; wild

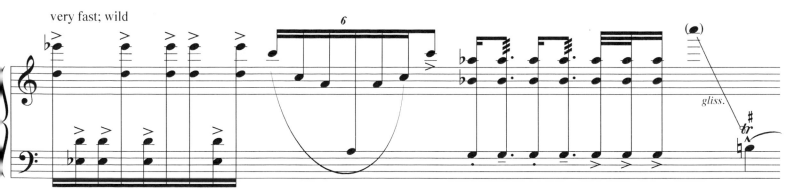

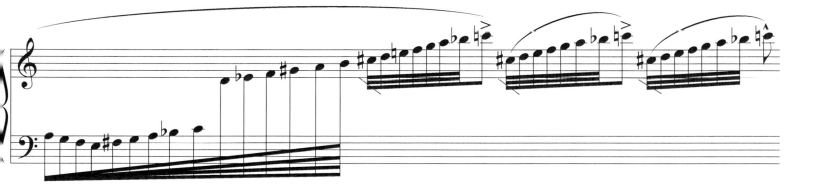

noticeably in a strict,
"pompous" tempo

♩=ca. 69

♩=92 in the new tempo for "Woodrag"

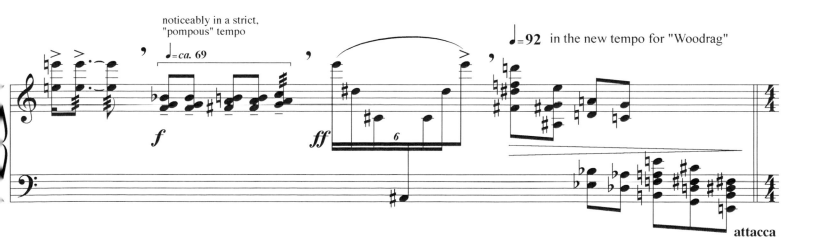

attacca

Woodrag

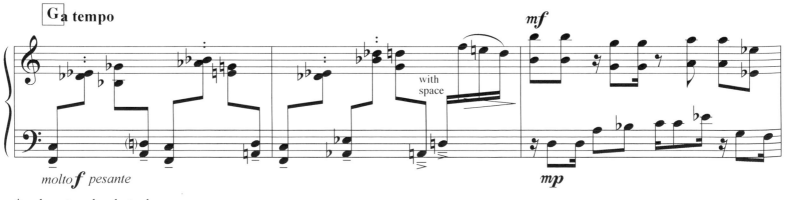

* : denotes dead stroke

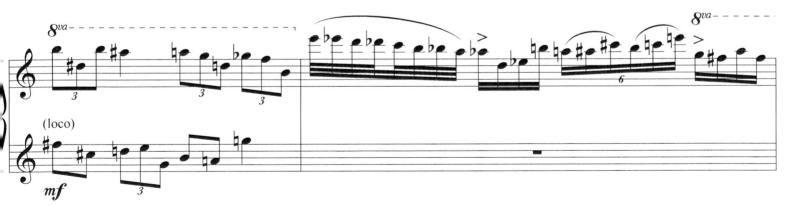

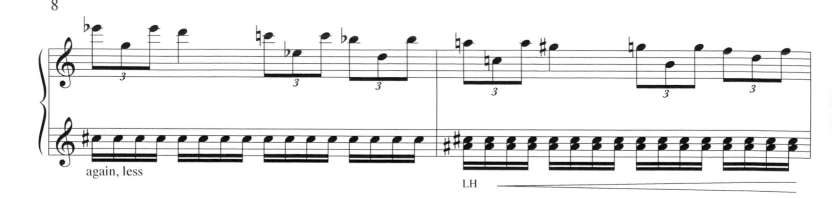

again, less   LH

I

ff   mf

ossia: 8va lower

f

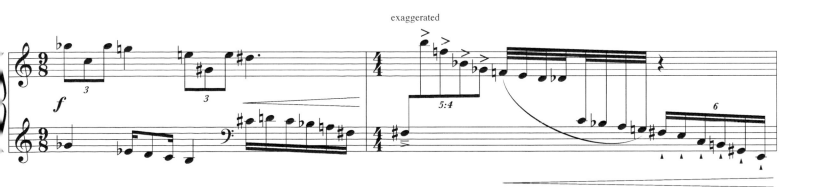

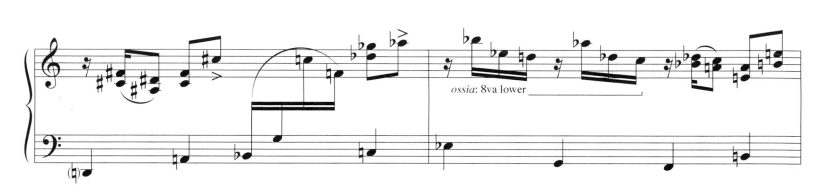

II

Pastorale

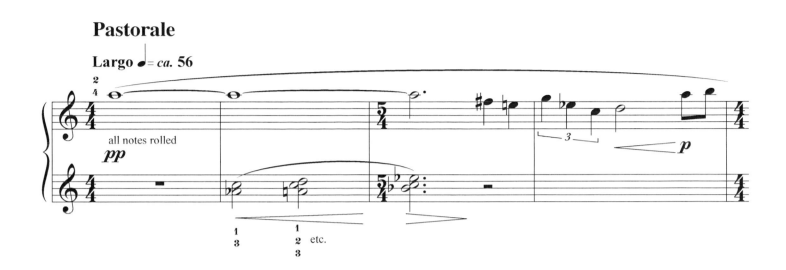

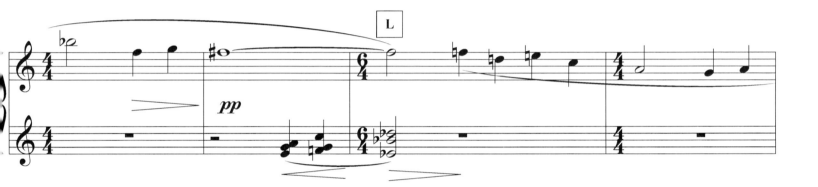

a sudden outburst
(not rolled)

M all rolled again

Forked Road

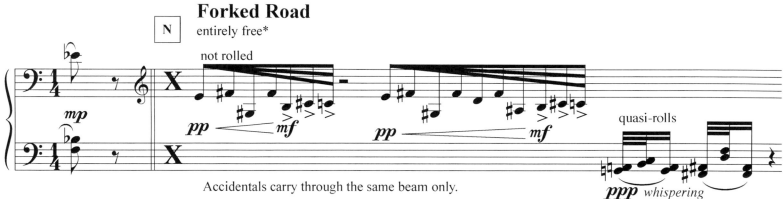

Accidentals carry through the same beam only.

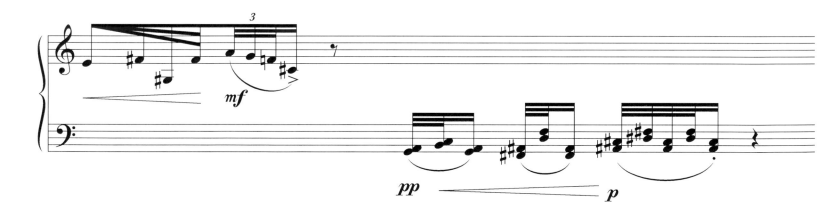

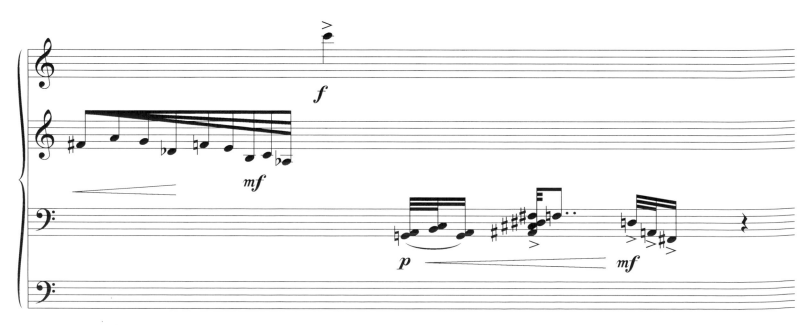

*Do not attempt to strictly match the rhythms of each individual staff to another. Keep events moving, but observe rests. Better to move from event to event (staff to staff) too quickly than too slowly, yet play it as you feel it. Each of the four staves is to be thought of as a separate line, and should retain its character.

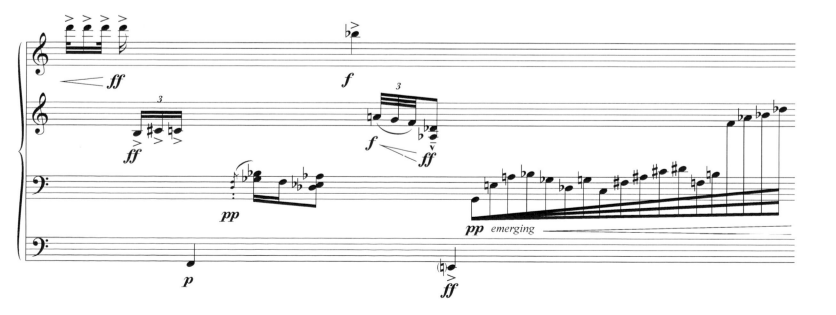

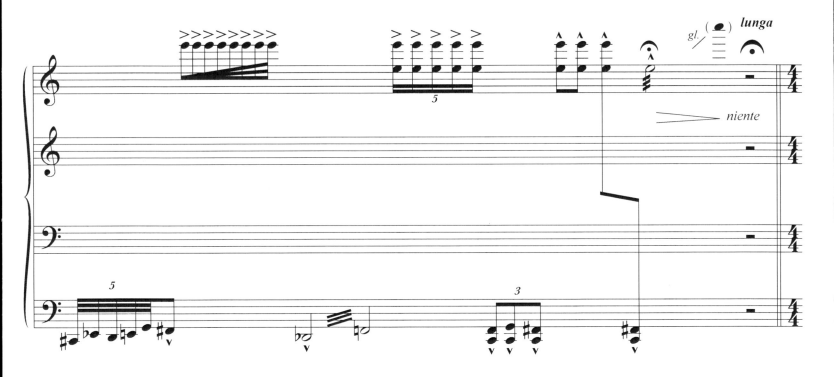

Echo

O Tempo I

all notes rolled

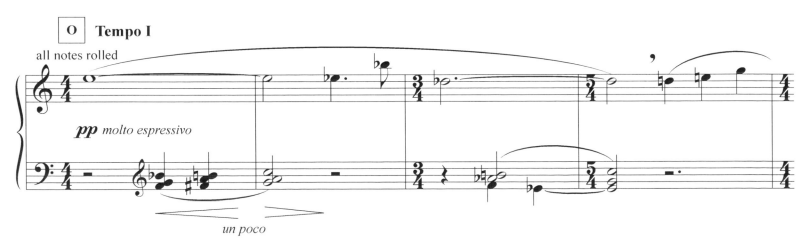

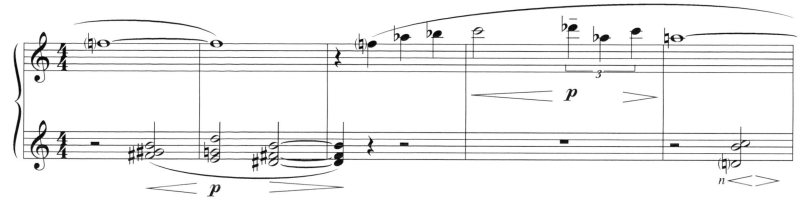

P **Slightly faster and less expressive;** *placid and medieval*

LH not rolled

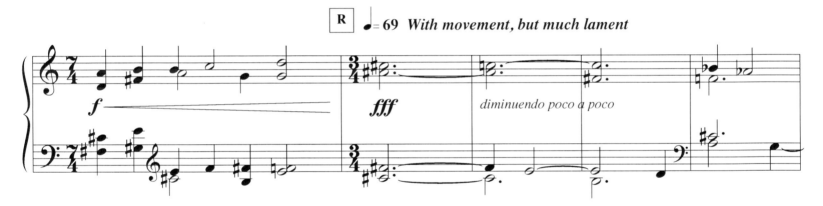

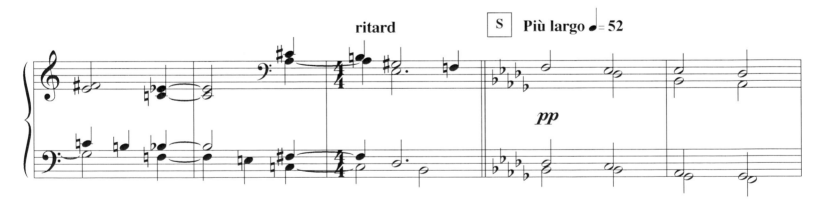

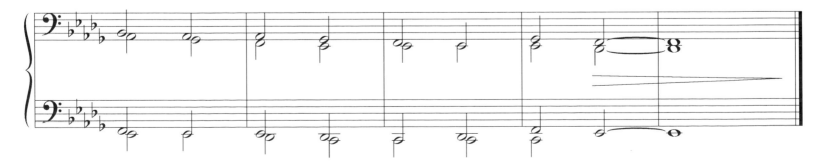

III

Plain Dance

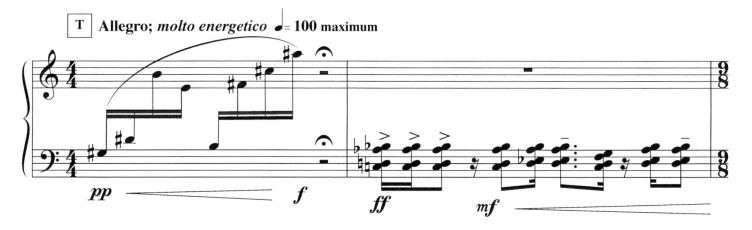

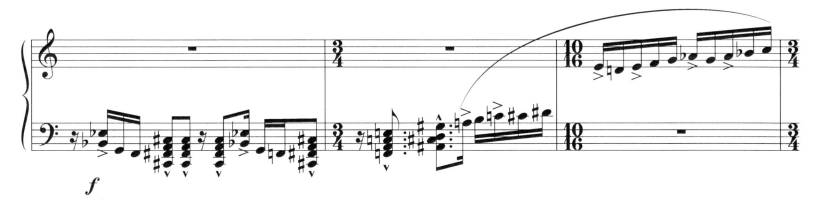

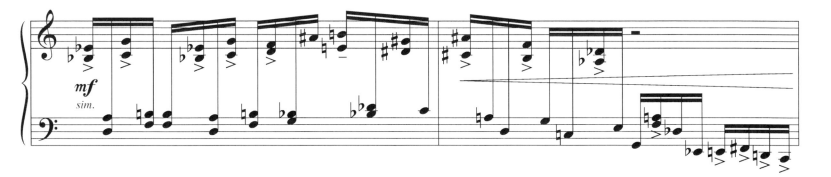

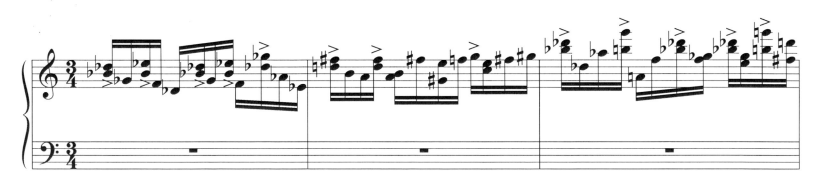

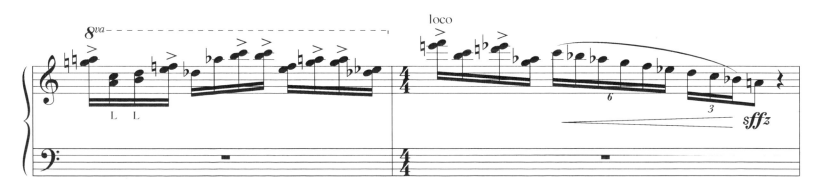

W Resume; calmer

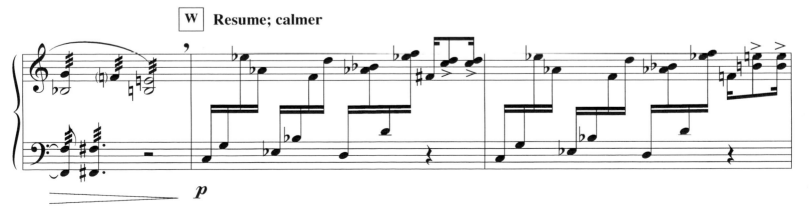

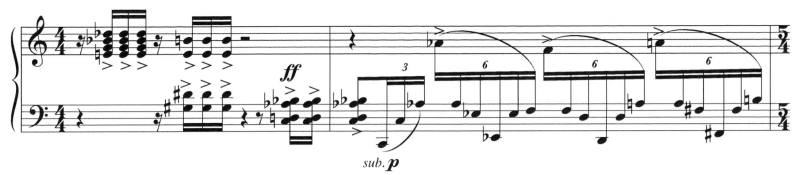

A tempo

Z *lyrical, romantic*

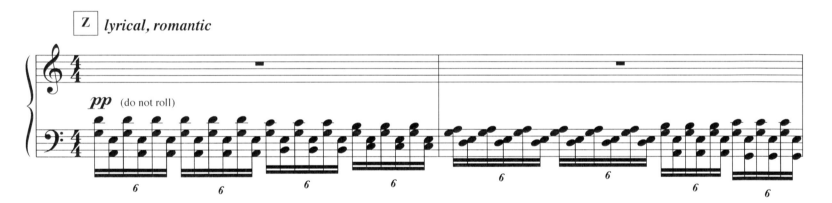

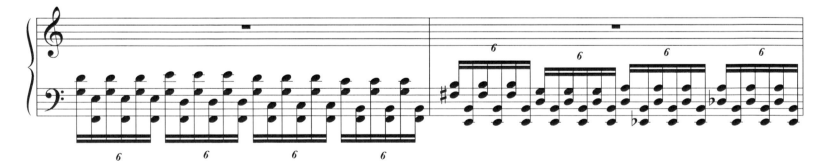

begin very gradual crescendo

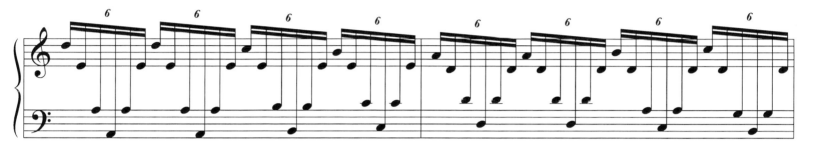

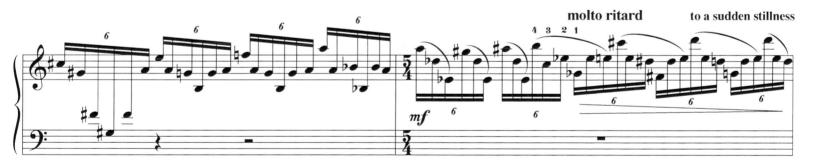

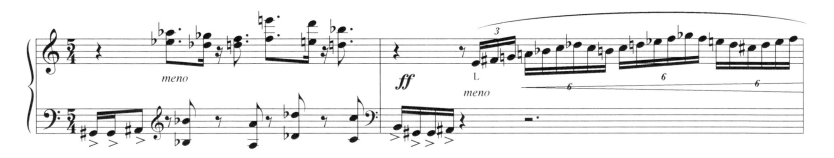

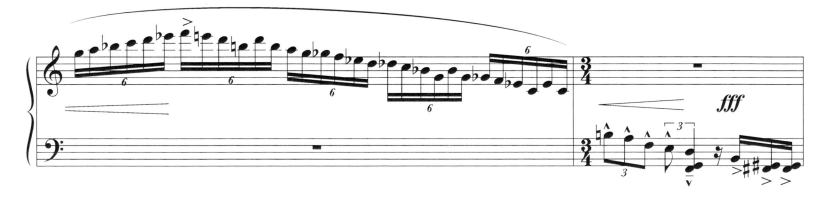

March, 1991
Ann Arbor